I have never read a memoir _____
Autobiography of a Baby, *Pa*_____
*poems from birth to fourteen mo*_____
*so powerful that I long to pick up t___ ____ ___ hug him until
the "deep hole of pain" and "the raw sob" are gone. Readers
cannot escape the pathos in Reardon's memoir, or the "line"
from his Aunt running deep in the baby. The Aunt who
holds him close. The Aunt who calls him "Puddin'."*

—Sandra Fluck
Editor of The Write Launch arts website

*It's not easy being a baby...finding your voice, finding your
way, finding your place in the world. Patrick T. Reardon
brings his reportorial skills and clear writing style to the
challenges of the world through a baby's eyes. You will
take Puddin' into your arms and into your heart...which
will be broken and made whole again over and over as you
read his story, and then when you read the story behind it.*

—Charles Dickinson
Author of the forthcoming novel, *Stan_Dalone*

*Patrick T. Reardon has written a powerfully imagined
book. From the moment we encounter the first three words
of Puddin'—she is gone—the simplicity of the language
sweeps us into the narrative like a great river in search of
its source. The journey here is not one that depends on our
skill or ability to navigate unfamiliar waters. Rather, it
sets us down in the center of a slow-moving whirlpool and
beckons us to share the heartbreaking genuineness at the
core of this remarkable memoir.*

—Paul Fericano
Author of The Suicide Notes and Things That Go Trump in the Night

Puddin'

Puddin'

THE AUTOBIOGRAPHY OF A BABY
A MEMOIR IN PROSE POEMS

PATRICK T. REARDON
FOREWORD BY HAKI R. MADHUBUTI

THIRD WORLD PRESS

PROGRESSIVE BLACK PUBLISHING SINCE 1967

CHICAGO

Third World Press
Publishers since 1967
Chicago

Third World Press
P.O. Box 19730,
Chicago, IL 60619

Cover photo: Thinkart, Dreamstime.com
Cover design concept: David Joseph Shiel Reardon
Cover and interior layout and design: Denise Borel Billups

First Edition
Printed in the United States of America
ISBN: 978-0-88378-425-9 | Paperback
27 26 25 24 23 22   7 6 5 4 3 2 1

Dedicated to Sarah, John, Tara, David and
Emmaline and Ulysses
and, as always,
Cathy

In memory of Mary Fitzgerald
and Mary Thomas

Foreword

Patrick T. Reardon's Puddin: The Autobiography of a Baby, A Memoir in Prose Poems is a literary first, and most likely a last of its kind. Reardon would have it that babies do talk to themselves and have advanced thoughts and see the world beyond their birth to 14 months-old.

Reason would have it, that to an ill-informed mind babies are just babies, especially at that age and exist to drink mother's milk, sleep long hours, cry, dirty their diapers and start over again several times each day. However, the beauty of the creative spirit, the insight of a learned, conflicted, and searching mind can and will be adventurous in their telling of the exploratory wonderment of the first year of life.

This reimagining of one's first year gives the reader a baby's chronicle into the deep possibilities of an untold life. The mere thought of writing as one's infant self is not only a first in poetry, most probably a first in book form. As I read this highly-creative and fascinating work, consuming it primarily as a poet myself, I thought *how in the hell did somebody come up with an idea like this?* From the first page entitled "January 3rd 1950," I was introduced to Puddin's inquisitive, yet sparse vocabulary: "She is gone. I wish I knew why she goes." Here, a baby wonders about the disappearance of his mother between routine diaper changes and bottle feedings. The child goes on to reveal how observant we are at that stage of life by taking note of fine details such as the roughness of his mother's hands juxtaposed against the "smoothness of the thing that holds the milk."

In another poem, "Sixty-Five," baby is blanketed in the love of a dear Aunt who takes precious care of him while mother and father are away:

> Aunt feeds me with the spoon. I make my
> mouth wide to take in the food. Aunt says
> words to me. I hear Puddin. I smile. She and
> he are out.

There is no sharper insider view than the first-hand account Reardon provides through an illuminating lens of prose poetry. In this collection, Reardon does not underestimate the perceptive nature of newborns. Reardon does well to highlight a series of developmental (dimensions) milestones surrounding a baby's journey into their sense of voice, identity, struggle and triumph. Nearly each day covered is written as a journal entry documenting a baby's sensory experiences. It's imaginative and it takes imagination to decipher this work and to understand it in its uniqueness and simplicity of both form and language. What is required of the reader is to put aside all he or she has learned in the construction of fictional poetry that does not conform to everyday conversation or writing.

Puddin' meets our curiosity head on with vigorous originality and vibrant memory recall. Stretching itself out of a womb of wonder into a realm of prose poems that embark upon uncharted territory—baby talk. A language all its own. A language that could only be translated by a poet poised with the skills to bring a genuine portrait of the joy and pain surrounding birthing a child to natural light. Reardon's signature reportage style alone magnificently moves this collection and breathes new life into the literary universe.

Reading the afterword does help to bring into perspective the human journey that Reardon had to absorb, analyze and come to grips with before writing this important work. That he was one of fourteen children with a father who was a policeman earning a yearly salary that barely made ends meet speaks loudly to the demands of the Catholic Church regarding birth control. His mother worked miracles and is to be understood as a loving parent who did all she could in between pregnancies and child rearing. On the streets, there is a highly patriarchal saying, whether serious or not, that claims the *best way to control women is to keep them barefooted and pregnant.*

As a publisher, editor, and poet for over fifty-five years, and also an educator of literature and writing for forty-two years, I have never come across a memoir of this power, attractiveness, creativity and formative intuition. Reardon has given rebirth to a retelling of his mother's and aunt's *Puddin'*. Fertile ground, yes. Original avenues, yes. Inventive and ingenious in his narration. The primary incentive (impulse) for my writing this brief publisher's note, which I've only done once in the history of Third World Press, is that I was surprisingly impressed with this one-year memoir. That Patrick Reardon is not of my culture provides a greater gift for me in understanding his culture. Read, enjoy and let us hear from you.

—Haki Madhubuti, MFA, Ph.D.,
University Distinguished Professor Emeritus
Chicago State University, Founder of Third Word Press

Puddin'

ONE
January 3, 1950

She is gone. I wish I knew why she goes. She was not glad I shit. She made that face. Her hands were rough as she changed me. She tied the strap more tight on me and put the milk thing through my lips with force. I feel the smooth skin of the thing that holds the milk. It is slick. The tips of my hands stretch out. They hurt and feel good. I want to cry. The milk wants to get in my mouth. The brown tip feels wrong. I won't suck. I have no way to cry. I scrunch my eyes. I send lines through me. They are lines of light in me. There are lines of fire. I move my legs. I jerk them. I want her to come back. I do not want her to come back.

January 6, 1950

He is here. He keeps his space. He looks to her. He has that frown. He has that line to his mouth. He does not like to look at me. His hands are large. They move me with ease. He smiles when she is here. He makes jokes. He flies me bare through the air. The breeze is cold on my skin. I pee. They laugh.

January 10, 1950

Aunt's eyes smile. Her voice smiles. My eyes go wide with joy. The skin of her face is soft on the skin of my face. I feel her and lean all of me on her. She hugs me on her. The weight of her arms feels good, like I am part of her. The length of her on the length of me feels good. I look at her eyes. They look at me. A line runs from her eyes through mine to deep in me. She calls me Puddin'.

January 29, 1950

In the dark, I keen for that which has no name. From deep in my throat, I bring forth sharp sound. I rage at the blank lack. I know she will not come. He will not come. I know I will go through the dark and then, with light, she or he will come. Most nights, I do not roil. Most nights, I keep in my skin. I hold fire. I bide time. Now, I mourn with loud cry. I grieve with raw sob.

February 8, 1950

The sound in the air makes me feel full. I am whole with the sound. I am calm. I ride the sound. It is a wind but in my ear. I am in the hug of sound. I am in its warm hug. The sound comes from the brown box. She comes in the room. She does her work. She uses her voice to ride the sound, too. She aims her voice at me. Her eyes look at me but do not see me. I ride her voice. She has a smile on her face. I am one with her and the sound. A new sound, a new smile. She sings at the sink as she washes the plates and dries them. She hangs the towel on the rack. She goes to the brown box. The sound stops.

February 13, 1950

In the dark, in their bed in their room, they make sounds that scare me.

March 7, 1950

She moves chairs and all the rest. She talks to me as if I am her. I can tell that she is mad about what he said last night as they sat in their chairs at the meal. She moves lamps and stands. She moves the couch. She makes a new room. Her breath is hard in her chest, and there is sweat on her dress as she stands still to look at her work. She lights a smoke. She sits in a chair. She cries.

March 18, 1950

She changes my cloth wrap with sharp, clean moves. She hums and smokes. He is not as fast. She wipes me. The air on me feels cool. It is good when the wrap is wrapped. I am put in the cloth thing. My arms and my legs are put in the cloth thing. I am snapped tight. They lay me down and turn off the light. I feel the warm cloth thing hug me. I move here and there, stretch and reach, to make it hug me even more.

April 5, 1950

In my mind, I see that kid who crawled on the floor. I try to get how he did it. On the cloth on the rug, I am on my back. I roll, and I am on my front. I push my arms and legs on the cloth, and my butt is in the air. I do not move. I do not get it. I fill with mad.

April 22, 1950

The milk thing is in my mouth. The strap is tight on me. She sings as she gets dressed for their date. She walks in the room from the bath. Her breasts are bare. I yearn.

April 25, 1950

I will not eat. I will not eat. I will not eat.
I will not eat. I will not eat. I will not eat.
I will not eat. I will not eat. I will not eat.
I will not eat. I will not eat. I will not eat.
I will not eat. I will not eat. I will not eat.
I will not eat. I will not eat. I will not eat.
I will not eat. I will not eat. I will not eat.
I will not eat. I will not eat. I will not eat.
I will not eat. I will not eat. I will not eat.
I will not eat. I will not eat. I will not eat.
I will not eat. I will not eat. I will not eat.
I will not eat. I will not eat. I will not eat.
I will not eat. I will not eat. I will not eat.
I will not eat. I will not eat. I will not eat.
I will not eat. I will not eat. I will not eat.
I will not eat. I will not eat. I will not eat.
I will not eat. I will not eat. I will not eat.
I will not eat. I will not eat. I will not eat.

April 28, 1950

Aunt picks me up and hugs me to her neck. She takes me down the steps from the flat to the door and out to the street. She holds me. I look out at the world. She puts me in the push thing. We go down the street, turn, go down the street, turn, go down the street, turn, go down the street, turn, and we are back at the start. She picks me up and holds me. I look out at the world. My eyes look at what I do not know. So wide. So high. So loud. So full. So much. It nerves me and calms me, too. I store it. Each piece must fit. I know each piece must fit. I know. I will find a way to fit them.

April 30, 1950

I chew my hand and the parts of my hand, and drool runs down to my wrist and on the cloth that I lay on. I gnaw at my hand with bare gums. The gums ache. When I chew my hand, they feel good and bad. She comes in and wipes my face and hand and wrist with a soft cloth. She gives me a soft dog to chew. She leaves the room.

May 2, 1950

They put his hat on me. They smile at me. I look at them. Am I him? I want to be him. I want her to see me as she sees him. I move. The hat falls. They laugh. What did I do?

May 4, 1950

He reads the sheets of words in his chair by the lamp. She is in her chair. She reads a book. I am on the cloth on the floor. I drool.

May 6, 1950

Words come from the brown box. It is a man's voice. He speaks as if he knows. He says words that start, move and end. There is the sound of fast clicks in the back of the sound. I do not know what the words mean. I hear the beat of the words from his voice and feel it in my skin and in my brain. They pour down to a part of my brain where I keep things.

May 10, 1950

He is at the edge at all times. She is close and large and full of strength. I reach, reach, reach for her.

May 11, 1950

I chafe. I ache. I have a fire line down and up my spine. In the crib, I whine in a soft, wet way. She moves through the flat on quick steps. I smell the food in the cook room. I whine. She picks me up and holds me out from her. She holds me with her hands. I chafe. I ache. She checks my cloth wrap. She puts me down.

May 13, 1950

I am on the cloth on the rug on my back. I roll, and it scares me. I give a cry or two and stop. I roll to the right a bit. I roll to the left a bit. I roll. I am on my front. I hold my head up and look. She comes in the room and puts me back on my back.

May 16, 1950

In a quick flash, she sets me on the rug and turns in the white room where she spews in the white bowl. At night, he walks in and comes to her and looks down to her and puts his hand on her waist. They smile. She cries. He holds her.

May 19, 1950

I am in a new place. Paw is here and Gram. Gram hugs me to her chest. I feel I will drown in her skin and her dress. Gram smells of the cook room. Paw has a sharp smell to him. His hair is tight. It is bright with oil. His lips smile. His eyes dart. She takes me from Gram and sets me on the cloth on the rug. No one else is here in this large room with dark chairs and wood that shines. Sun comes through the glass squares on the long wall. In the beam of the sun, I see small spots dance.

May 20, 1950

I feel pain here on my skin and there. It is small. There are lines of pain from my brain and down through all of me. My deep, deep place is tight and thick. It is a fist.

May 22, 1950

I hear Aunt in the flat. I smile. I know she will pick me up and smile at me and our eyes will lock. I know she will come in soon. I hear her. Now I do not hear her. He looks in my room. I stand in the crib. He goes.

May 23, 1950

Look at me! Look at me! Look at me! Look
at me! Look at me! Look at me! Look at
me! Look at me! Look at me! Look at me!
Look at me! Look at me! Look at me! Look
at me! Look at me! Look at me! Look at
me! Look at me! Look at me! Look at me!
Look at me! Look at me! Look at me! Look
at me! Look at me! Look at me! Look at
me! Look at me! Look at me! Look at me!
Look at me! Look at me! Look at me! Look
at me! Look at me! Look at me! Look at
me! Look at me! Look at me! Look at me!
Look at me! Look at me! Look at me! Look
at me! Look at me! Look at me! Look at
me! Look at me! Look at me! Look at me!
Look at me! Look at me! Look at me! Look
at me! Look at me! Look at me! Look at
me! Look at me! Look at me! Look at me!
Look at me! Look at me! Look at me! Look

May 26, 1950

She smokes as she talks on the phone. I know Gram is on the line. I don't know how I know. Her words have a beat — talk, not, talk, not, talk, not... There is a line from her out of the flat. It must touch Gram. When she talks to me, there is no beat. There is an edge to the words. There is an itch to the sounds.

TWENTY-SIX
May 26, 1950

I hear her tell Gram there will be a new child. A new me?

May 28, 1950

Paw grows tight when he is near me. Gram tells him to hold me. His skin seems to crunch up. He growls. I look in his eyes. He looks off.

May 30, 1950

A man with bright lights has come to the flat. They shine in my face. I blink and blink. He has a black box on legs. White cloth is put on one of the big chairs. She seats me in the midst of that white and puts a blue and white cloth over my legs. She props me up. The man with the lights is calm. He coos to me as he moves me a bit this way and a bit that way. He props me. He smiles at me. He makes fun. I smile. He looks in my eyes with fun. I smile. He locks eyes with me. I am filled with a smile. I hear clicks. Then, the lights go off. His smile goes off. The man packs the lights and the black box, too. She gives him some bills. He nods and thanks her. He leaves. She takes me to the crib and leaves the room. I blink. I blink.

June 3, 1950

Aunt has me on the grass in the park. I like the way each blade of grass points up. I like how all the blades are cool to my touch, soft and hard at the same time. The trees step to the sky. The sky has no end.

June 6, 1950

In the dark, I wake. I see the shades of dark.
I hear birds. Their sounds are lines from
one to the other. Their sounds are lines
from them to me. I close my eyes. I sleep.

June 10, 1950

She stomps back and forth on the floor. I cry. Her eyes dart at me. There is a fire line from those eyes to me. I cringe.

June 10, 1950

There is a loud noise in the cook room. I crane my neck to see. He comes in and looks at her. She must be on the floor. He kneels down to help her. She moves in some way, and he leans back. She cries mad.

June 19, 1950

She does not like Aunt.

June 22, 1950

He sews. He takes each cloth and runs the fast nail through it to make a line and sets it to the side. His face is taut as he looks sharp at each move he makes.

June 24, 1950

I am a deep hole of pain. I am full of mad.
I want to rage at her. I mourn for what I
do not know. She puts her face close to me
in the crib, and she is a god in rock. She
frowns at me. I look. She looks.

June 28, 1950

They have me in a big space, filled with gold and red and blue and green. She and he tell me: Hush! A coin falls on the wood, and I hear the sound rise to the height, through the roof, through the sky to the stars. It is a sharp sound, not like the strong tunes of the choir. I ride the coin sound up.

June 30, 1950

A fly zips to the right and to the left. I wait for her.

July 5, 1950

His voice is deep and slow. Hers is high and
sharp. When they talk, their words dance. I
watch. I take it in. I store it.

July 14, 1950

My eyes grow large when I see Aunt. My smile grows wide. I make sounds in my throat. I want to make a line to her. She calls me Puddin'. I want to say Aunt to her.

July 14, 1950

Aunt cries. She holds me to her. Her tears seem to open a door to what I want to know. I mourn to hear her cry. I am sad to see her tears. There is a line from her sad to my sad and back.

July 19, 1950

I fall and fall and fall. I jolt. My arms and my legs shake with one big spasm. My eyes jerk wide and deep in my skull. I am here, in the dark, in my crib. I cry out. I make sound, then sound, then sound, from my throat. In a slow way, I catch my breath. I breathe in and out. She will not come. He will not come. But this dark is safe. I know it. I sleep.

July 20, 1950

Her waist grows big. Her skin shines. Her eyes strain. She sits in her chair and smokes. She writes on a pad. She makes lists.

July 27, 1950

The sounds from the brown box have sense.
The words that she says to him and that he
says to her have sense. My eyes see the lines
of the world, and each leads to each. The
lines make one world. Smells have lines of
their own. They do not link. They fog me.
What is worse is the blank lack.

July 30, 1950

She sets me down on an odd rug in a flat I do not know. She says words to me. There are two kids here. They touch me and move me back and forth and grow bored. They play.   They leave me on the cloth on the rug. One crawls, one walks. I watch them. What does she want?

August 3, 1950

She looks deep in the wall as she sits in the chair in the cook room. Now and then, she turns to me in the high chair and puts the spoon in my lips. I take some. She looks at the wall. She is not in this room. She brings the spoon to my lips. This time, I turn my head. I cry. She wipes my face with a rough, wet cloth and puts me in the crib.

August 5, 1950

The blank lack weighs on me. This is a weight I have on my neck. I find a way to hold it on a point there. I keep the line flat and straight. It is the line of the land where the sun rises. It is stored there. I do not feel it most of the time.

August 10, 1950

He makes a stretch to touch the top of the door space. She gives him a thumb tack. He hangs the white cross there. They look at me and say some words. The sounds itch in my brain. I work to take the sounds in. I store the sounds. They leave the room. I hear birds out past the glass.

August 11, 1950

She holds me in the car as he drives. This is "fast." It is the sound to match the quick move through the air. She and he talk and then do not. I look at his face. His lips are in a line as he looks out the front. She stares to the right through the glass. My cloth wrap chafes.

August 15, 1950

Her smell is soft. His smell is tart. The smells reach out to me now and then. I reach to touch them. But the lines are thin and break with ease.

August 19, 1950

The bars of my crib are lines that fit with the other lines to make the crib. There is a line that I have been set on. It is a wall that I am flat on. The bars form a wall on one side and on the other. There is a wall at the foot and head of the crib. A wall, a wall, a wall, a wall and a wall. There is no wall up there where my eyes go when I look to the top of the room.

August 20, 1950

He comes in the door in his blue with the star on his chest. He is tall. He is more tall than she is. He is a lot more tall. He takes the few steps to her, wraps her in his arms, bends her, leans her back and gives her a kiss on the lips. Her eyes close. His eyes close. Their eyes open. Their eyes lock. As they move, he sees me as I look at them. He takes his thumb on my chin and moves my chin up and down as if I am talking to them. They laugh. Her hand is in touch with the skin of his arm. They leave the room.

August 20, 1950

I am worn out. She and he talk with wide
eyes at the meal in the cook room. I fussed
but gave in and ate. I gaze now back and
forth. She says more than he does. I have
sought the key to the lock of the door of the
two of them. I have tried this way and that
way to find the code. My eyes blink, and
blink, and blink.

August 24, 1950

Aunt wears a smooth, soft top. The light leaps from her long hair and from her bright white smile. The art in the church has men who look like her. They have wings. They lead to God. Aunt told me about God.

August 25, 1950

I fly on the sound from the brown box. She sleeps in her chair. I look out the glass and ride the sound out in the world — down the street, past the trees. I look down at the cars as they move. I see the grass. I see the trash. I ride the breeze of the tune through the sky. I sleep.

September 3, 1950

She has dark hair and sharp moves. She keeps her self to her self.

September 5, 1950

I swim in a wet weight. Sweat is thick on my skin. My head is hot. She puts a new cloth wrap on me. She puts drops in my mouth. I ache. I spew. I take the ache and put it in a room. I close the door. I live here to keep from the room with the ache. I live here where I can take in the play of light on the glass of the brown case and push to know what the lights mean. I know I must not spew. I know I must not cry.

September 8, 1950

She has me in the push thing. She stops to smoke and look at the bed of green and white and red. A man with red hair walks by. His dog barks. I jerk. I fear. All of me snaps, from my toes to my hair. All of my skin snaps. I cry. She says words to me from her height and strength. I shake but do not cry more. I breathe. In time, I grow calm.

September 9, 1950

She sobs. I can hear her from here. What makes her sad? Does she know the void? Does she know the blank lack? I do not cry. I make no sound. I hold my breath.

September 12, 1950

She and he have guests this night in the flat. There are kids. There are big ones, too. He smokes a pipe and has a beer. The men stand to one side and talk in deep voices. Her eyes are sharp as she sits with the wives in the soft chairs. She says a lot and laughs a lot. All light bends to her. When she is not the one to speak, she reads her own skull. I can tell. He makes odd sounds. The big ones laugh. I watch two kids crawl. I push and lift and move in some way and gain ground. My arms and legs move on their own. She says words at me and, in her chair, fakes that she is the one who crawls. I don't know what she means. She laughs.

September 15,1950

It is dark now. She and he have gone. But Aunt is here. I try not to sleep, but I sleep. I wake when they come back. Their eyes glow. Her head bends to him. His head bends to her. They look at me. I look back. They leave the room.

September 17, 1950

I look at the space where the couch stops, the space down to the floor. It is a space where there is dust and a small metal thing like an odd bowl. I reach and strain, but my hand stays too far from the space. I want to cry, but then she will move me to the crib.

September 18, 1950

His stone face does not let me in.

September 24, 1950

In the heat, I sweat. I know this is "hot."
She and he sit on the porch when the sun
is gone. I am in the sit thing that squeaks
when I bounce. The slim wind is warm on
top of warm. They talk.

September 30, 1950

He is in the cook room at the sink to wash
the plates. His back is a tall, wide hill that
I see go up, up, up. It is a flat, blank hill. It
is all strength, all weight. It has no sound.

October 1, 1950

Aunt feeds me with the spoon. I make my mouth wide to take in the food. Aunt says words to me. I hear Puddin'. I smile. She and he are out.

October 4, 1950

The new sun comes through the glass in the wall. She and he move here and there. He is in his blue with the star. She is in her robe. He leans down to kiss her. The line from her to him, from him to her is strong and thick. When he goes out the door, the line is still there. It can stretch from her to him, from him to her as far as it needs to.

October 6, 1950

The sounds from the brown box show how things can be right. The sounds move. They are a road through time. They are right. They are the green and brown of a tree. They are right. They are Aunt's smile. The tune hugs me. I ride the tune. I am up from the blank lack, the thing with no name.

October 7, 1950

His legs are like trees as he steps past me on the rug where I crawl and drool. Spit runs down my chin. She puts a dry cloth on my face to wipe it. I do not shake my head any more. I let her wipe. I want to stay on the rug.

October 12, 1950

In my crib, I make sounds in my mouth in a soft way. I hear the sounds in my head. I try to match the sounds that I have stored there. They are words. I hear the sound "food" in my head, but do not know how to make my mouth make the sound. She says words to me and leaves the room.

October 19, 1950

The cloth dog is lost. I am deep sad. I want
to hope. I think there is a way for me to
find it. I need to look hard. I keep my eyes
wide. I search as I can. I look to her. I look
to him. I cry. I stop.

October 20, 1950

She sings with the brown box. She dances to the tune. She is all that is bright in the world. I watch. I yearn.

October 22, 1950

She and he have me in church. No one is in the pews. Most of the big space is dark. The lack of sound is loud. He stands in the back. He is at the back of the group of big ones near the bowl of wet. I am in his arms in a way that does not fit well. She stands next to the bowl with Gram and Paw. Two big ones hold a new child. A man in robes pours wet on the head of the child. The child cries. I am not sure if I want to cry. Light comes in through the red, blue, green and white glass. I want to fly up to the light. I want to fill this great space.

October 28, 1950

Gram gives me sweet crumbs. She limps to the stove in her cook room. She says a loud word to me and stands in the way as she takes a tray out of the stove. She smiles at me.

October 29, 1950

I set my blocks on the rug near me. She says some words to me and takes a block. I reach for it. She holds it back and says some words. She takes more blocks. I reach for them. She says some words and holds them back. I want to cry but do not. I look at her.

November 1, 1950

She naps. He reads the sheets full of words
as he sits in the chair near the lamp. I crawl
the floor. At the couch, I climb up the wood
to stand. I look here and there. I look up at
the wall of sheets in front of his face.

November 2, 1950

It is night. He is not here. He wore his blue and star and went out to work. In the dark past the glass, I hear a loud noise. Her eyes get thin. She thinks this is a bad thing. I can tell. She leaves the lights on.

November 3, 1950

He comes in the door, and I can feel the cold that comes in with him. There is snow on his boots and snow on his hat. His coat is wet with snow. He takes off his boots. He takes off his hat and his coat. He walks to her, bends her over and gives her a kiss. She laughs and says words soft in his ear.

SEVENTY-EIGHT
November 9, 1950

My eyes pop wide. I am in the crib. I do not
know where I was. A scene fades. I was a
big one. I was a small one. I was a fly. I
was in the cook room with her. There was
a smell that hurt my nose.

November 11, 1950

The trees are brown. The wind is cold.
The grass is gray. Big flakes of snow start to
fall fast as Aunt picks me up out of the push
thing and hugs me close and says, Puddin',
as she walks up the stairs to the flat. There,
Aunt hands me to her. She takes me to the
white room and gives me a bath. She has a
hard time when she bends at the side of the
tub. Her waist gets wide each day. She puts
me in the long wrap for bed. I yawn. On
the way to the crib, she stops at the glass in
the wall and looks out on the world which is
thick and white with the new snow. I stare.

November 12, 1950

The big one in black and white robes has a soft smile for me. She smells like the white room. Part of the cloth she wears is hard. She holds my hand as I take some steps. She is in a room with rows of desks. I step from desk to desk. I laugh. He gives her a smile that is off to the side. I am not sure why. She waves as he drives the car past her on the way back to the flat.

November 15, 1950

She and he fight with words. His voice is loud and deep. Her voice is high and loud. The sounds lash back and forth. I tense.

November 15, 1950

In deep night, I wake up in the dark and can see in the shades of dark that she is on the couch. I can hear her as she cries. He sits next to her. He says no words. He does not touch her. He sits. She cries. Her tears wet her face. Her breath slows down. Her sobs get soft. She turns to him. She talks. He talks. They hug.

November 21, 1950

She is fat now. I know a new child will come. The new child will live here, too. She and he talk. They put a crib next to my crib. I am at the point of a tall hill and fear to fall.

November 22, 1950

In my crib, I fear. I feel bare. I am a scream no one can hear. I scrunch up at the end of the crib. I try to be small. I fill with fear. I wait. I wait. I wait.

November 26, 1950

A lot of big ones and kids are here in the flat. They look at me. I look at them. I am not sure what to do. This big one holds me and then turns to pass me on to the next. And I am passed one more time. One sets me down on the cloth on the floor, and I start to crawl. Soon, she picks me up and puts me in the high chair in the big room. All of the big ones and kids are in there. They all look at me and at the cake with a stick topped with a fire. They turn off the light and sing. I look at them. I am not sure what to do. I want to cry but know not to. He puts a piece of cake on my plate and turns.

December 11, 1950

I am in his arms as he stands at the bar in the dark room with men who smile wide and talk loud and laugh loud. He is tall and looks down at the men before him. In his arms, I can look right in the face of each man. Each face draws me in. The smell here is tart and taut. He says we are on our way out. Each man shakes his hand. He pulls the door, and I blink, blink, blink at the strong, bright sun. The cold wind hits my face.

December 11, 1950

In the night, I wake in the dark. I am sad and spent. I look at the shades of light and dark. In those shades, I see lines I have not seen. I trace one line from here to there. I see it meets a line that goes in that way. There are a lot of lines on the front of the brown case. I see that the lines meet in a way that is right. They fit. I see lines all through the room. I ride each line from its start to its end. I fill with joy.

December 21, 1950

He bangs the nail in the wall. I move to see him close. He sees me. His eyes are mad. He says words to her. She picks me up and takes me to the big room. She hands me the book with the dogs and cats. Aunt gave me the book. I know the black things are words. There are words in the sheets that he reads in his chair and in the book she reads in her chair. She says words to me. Her hands say to me to stay here.

December 24, 1950

In the dark, we go from the car through the snow in the church. She and he meet Aunt in the back, and Gram and Paw, too, and some big ones I don't know. I smell the smoke that comes from the front. It is not a smell I know. It puts an itch in my nose in a way I like. I hear the song from the choir up in the back. The big ones sing the song. There is a deep sound to the song that I can feel in my skin. I feel it deep to my bones. Aunt smiles to me. She says Puddin'. The man in the robes says words in a beat that moves in a way that I want to ride. The words hold the smell and the song and the high, high height here. The lines fit.

December 27, 1950

In the flat, she moves back and forth with sharp steps. She shifts the chairs and the couch in the big room. I try to get in. She keeps me out. I try. She keeps me out. I try. She keeps me out. I try. She picks me up in a fierce way and puts me in the crib. I cry as loud as I can. I am full of mad. I cry from deep in my throat. I cry. I cry. I cry. I rage. I am full of mad. My face is hot. I tire. I gulp for breath. I tire. I lay down. I sleep.

December 29, 1950

I see the line that runs from Gram to Paw and from Paw to Gram. It is a line that has bumps and frail parts. I want a line that is strong that I can share. I need to be a big one for that. But I have a line to Aunt when I see her.

January 1, 1951

In the big room, there is a piece of cloth that is part of the couch on the edge of the wood line. This piece of cloth has a feel that I like. Each time I am in the big room, I touch the piece of cloth. The cloth feels brisk on the skin of my hand. It feels sharp in a soft way. It feels right in a way I have no way to say. It fits.

January 6, 1951

I like to crawl in the cook room where I can hear each time my hand hits the floor. In the big room, on the rug, I like to move from the couch to the chair. I pick up a small brass bowl for smokes and chew on it. My drool falls from my chin down to the glass of the side stand. I put my hand in the drool and move it on the glass to make forms. She makes that face and takes the bowl from me. She wipes my wet skin with a cloth that is dry and rough. She wipes the glass on the side stand.

January 7, 1951

Gram and Paw are here. Aunt is here, too.
Kids and big ones. There is a big crowd in
the flat. She sits in the big chair and talks
and smokes and sips the black drink. He
stands off to the side and keeps a close eye
on her. She takes a cloth thing out of a box
and holds it up and says words. The big
ones laugh. It is too small for me.

January 11, 1951

I hear her in the cook room. She gets the meal set. I lay in the crib. I curl up. I don't watch. She picks me up and puts me in the high chair. She and he talk. I sit and look out the glass, but I do not see the glass or what is past it. I glimpse the blank lack. I do not eat. They stop their words. She puts her hand on the top of my face. Her skin is soft, but I do not care. I fill with bleak and weight and pain. She puts drops in my mouth and puts me back in the crib. She sits down with him for the rest of the meal.

January 13, 1951

Aunt shows me a gold piece on a chain. The light shines on it in a new way with each turn it takes. I reach for it. I touch it. It is smooth. I want to grab it in my hand. Aunt won't let me. She smiles at me and says words. She says Puddin' to me. She puts the chain back on her neck. I see the gold on the blue of her blouse.

January 16, 1951

The light from the sun moves along the wall as I watch. It is here, and then it is there, and then it is there. The lamp is like the sun, but it does not move. The lamp goes from light to dark in a snap. The light of the sun comes out of the dark in a slow way and moves to dark in a slow way. I start to see how the world fits. I know there is a line from the sun in through the glass to this room. I know there is a line from the lamp to me when it is on. Do I send a line out to the sun? Do I send a line out to the lamp?

January 19, 1951

She and he talk soft. Then, they turn and say words to me. I look at them. I use my eyes to ask what they mean. They say more words. They make moves that say I am a big one. I'm not a big one. I shit. She makes the mad face. I am strong. She wipes me hard and puts on me a new cloth wrap and drops me in the crib. I jolt. I am weak.

January 21, 1951

Those kids on the stairs in front of the flat are loud and big and laugh a lot. They push and they bounce on the wall. They move fast. I see them through the door as she gets the mail. I want her back in the flat. I want her gone.

January 27, 1951

Aunt calls me Puddin', and we play a game with our hands. I slap her hand as fast as I can. She pulls her hands back, but most of the time I can get to her hands and make a loud noise of my skin on her skin. I laugh at the loud noise. I laugh at her wide smile. She touches me in the side, and it feels fun, and I laugh. She does it, I laugh. She does it, I laugh. She does it, I laugh. I can feel a smile wide on my face when I hear the sound on the stairs. They are on their way up to the flat. I feel the blank lack. I want to scream, but I know better. I blink, I blink.

January 28, 1951

I wake. In the dark, in this room, in the
new crib next to mine is the new child. His
name is David.

Afterword

At three in the morning, a few days before Thanksgiving in 2015, my brother David, tormented by unrelenting pain, groped his way out the back door of his suburban home into a frigid rain-snow and took his life.

He had been born in January, 1951, a little over a year after me. He and I were the first children of our parents, David and Audrey, and we were followed by two brothers and ten sisters. As adults, the fourteen of us remained close, all living in and around Chicago and gathering at regular intervals throughout the year for family parties.

David's suicide was a profound shock to those of us he left behind. And it wasn't.

Throughout his sixty-four years, he'd often been troubled, easily angered and uncomfortable in his skin. He'd threatened suicide twenty-five years earlier. In his final ten days, the medicine that had helped keep great arthritis pain at bay suddenly stopped working. His days and nights were filled with agony.

David's suicide led me to undertake a journey of my own to understand my brother and me and our relationship and our parents and our common history and our disparate life trajectories.

Puddin': The Autobiography of a Baby is a memoir. It's not fantasy. It is the story of a baby—me—during my first fourteen months, leading up to the birth of David. It's told from the perspective and in the voice of a baby. Each of this small book's 101 chapters is imagined. Yet, each is rooted in reality, in facts and feelings.

First, a word of background, I have been a news reporter of one sort or another since 1972. Most of my career, 32 years of it, was spent with the *Chicago Tribune* where I covered urban affairs, politics and the book industry.

I've been in psychotherapy twice. My first go-round lasted nearly the entire 1990s. Then, after David's suicide, I returned to my therapist.

In my earlier therapy, I had come to an understanding that our parents had developed a family system which had them at the center as the first and last word on all questions and as the focus of all affection. We were acolytes at their altar.

Now, though, I found that I needed to go deeper, not just to understand David's decision to take his life but all that led up to it in his life, in mine and in the lives of our sisters and brothers.

We children had all been taught and most still believed that Mom and Dad were just about the best parents possible. Even so, there was a general acknowledgement among us that they weren't "the touchy-feely type." After all, they were raising fourteen children on a policeman's salary! Who had time for hugs?

I wondered, though, if there had been a golden age when, with only one or two kids, they had been more nurturing. The problem was that there was no one I could turn to who could talk about how Mom and Dad were when I was their only child or when they were taking care of just David and me.

Our mother had died in 1995. Our father in 2003. None of their siblings was alive. Among my own brothers and sisters, David had been the one most likely to have memories going back far enough, but, during the 1990s, when I'd asked some questions, he refused to talk about any of Mom and Dad's flaws, insisting that they weren't perfect but were more than good enough.

As my second round of therapy went on, I began, almost without realizing it, to research the question in the only way I could find—by looking at the 40 or so black-and-white photos that our parents took of me during my first year and of David and me over the next couple of years.

I examined them closely, studying the expressions on the faces — not just of me and David but also of Dad and Mom and other relatives. I looked at the postures of the bodies, at how one body related to another, how one face looked at or away from another. I asked myself questions about why a certain photograph had been taken and about what scenes weren't recorded in the pictures. I related the photos to the emotions and memories that I carried that went into my early childhood although not to my infancy. I extrapolated.

It was the sort of educated guesswork I have done for so long as a reporter.

You gather facts and try to fit them together. In some cases, you can turn to someone who has already developed an explanation for the relationship of the facts to each other. But, often, in the sort of in-depth research in which I specialized at the Tribune, you have to synthesize the material and then, if the data warrant it, publish your findings in an accessible and coherent way.

That was the sort of approach I took in reporting on and writing about such subjects as the inequality of public school funding throughout Illinois, the middle-class migration out of the city, the social and cultural shifts behind the disappearance of the city's taverns, and the emotional, cultural and historical factors behind suburban sprawl. Employing this reporting method on my own life, though, was something I'd never consciously done before.

One striking thing that became quickly apparent when I studied the photographs from these earliest years was that David and I are never shown smiling.

There is one exception: A professional photo, tenderly colored with pastels by the photo studio. There, I have a big smile. So, it's clear that I knew how to smile.

There are also a couple shots in which I am being held by my Dad's sister, my Aunt Mary, who was my occasional babysitter. She's smiling, and, if I'm not exactly smiling, at least I'm not frowning.

Otherwise, in the photos, I am staring off into

space, and David is staring off into space if he's not crying with heavy emotion. There is one photo that shows David and me in his crib. He stands there keening with a great anger and hurt, and I'm behind him with this faraway look in my eyes.

After studying these photos, I came up with a term for that faraway look—the thousand-mile stare. I initially believed that I'd invented it myself, but, on second thought, I wondered if I might have heard it somewhere. So, I looked it up and quickly learned that it is a widely used term for the way soldiers appear when they are suffering from post-traumatic stress syndrome.

What I also noticed in the photos was that my Aunt Mary would clasp me close to her body and, often, close to her face. That wasn't the case with my mother or father.

My father apparently took most of these photographs, but, in a couple, you can see him holding me in his arms in an awkward way, as if he were a single man whom some friends had asked to carry their baby. That awkwardness is even more pronounced in the photos showing my mother with me or with me and David. She stands holding me in a way that seems designed to keep me away from her body, as if I had a bad smell. In other shots, she uses her arms to, literally, keep me and David at arm's length.

The photos—which had been carefully glued into a large black-page scrapbook by my mother and captioned with funny quips—are overwhelmingly sad for me to look at. But, through them, I had a window into my world as a baby and then with a baby brother.

As a reporter, I'm very aware of what I don't know. In this case, I don't know why my parents took these particular photos, these poses, these moments. My wife Cathy and I have two children, both now adults, and, if I pull out the photos that I took of them as babies, there are a few in which they're expressing discomfort. The vast, vast majority, though, show them smiling and playing and held close, face to face, body to body, with a widely smiling Cathy or me or the two of us.

Aside from the photos in the scrapbook, I don't know what the other moments of my babyhood looked like. It's possible, I guess, that there were times, not photographed, when David or I was smiling, or when our parents were playing with us. It's possible, but, as a reporter, I know that, human nature being what it is, it's not likely. Who photographs the depressing moments and ignores the happy ones?

But, then again, who photographs such depressing moments?

Because I'm a writer, I began to take what I was learning in therapy and from this research and put it into words, scribbled at first on fast-food restaurant napkins and then typed into my computer.

Some of those words became poems in my collection *Requiem for David*, published in 2017 by Silver Birch Press. Through these terse lines, I grappled with my feelings about David's suicide, about the way we were raised by my parents and about the closeness that I felt with all of my siblings despite the family system created and maintained by Mom and Dad. Of the sixty-two poems in the book, twenty-four were printed next to and in a kind of dialogue with one or more of the photos from my childhood.

Another product of my research is this memoir.

Let me answer a question that I am sure is going to be asked:

Yes, I know that, during a baby's first year, the infant does not think in the sort of words and concepts that I use here.

I also know, having watched the infancies of 13 siblings, two children of my own and scores of nieces and nephews and their children, as well as two grandchildren, that babies *do* think and feel and process the world in which they find themselves. They're not just lumps of protoplasm.

What I have sought to do here is to translate the inchoate thoughts and sensations of an infant—the specific infant who was me—into a language that hints at the simplicity and complexity of a baby's mind.

It is akin, I believe, to what William Faulkner did in his 1929 masterpiece *The Sound and the Fury* and, on a less elevated level, what W. Bruce Cameron did in his 2010 bestseller *A Dog's Purpose*. In both cases, the writers were attempting to translate the mental activity of two characters who would never have been able to read or understand the words that the authors put in their minds—Faulkner's mentally disabled Benjy ("Father went to the door and looked at us again. Then the dark came back, and he stood black in the door, and then the door turned black again.") and Cameron's mutt Toby ("One day it occurred to me that the warm, squeaky, smelly things squirming around next to me were my brothers and sisters. I was very disappointed.").

Yes, *Puddin': The Autobiography of a Baby* is fiction inasmuch as I have no documents or contemporary eyewitness accounts to point to the accuracy of my description of what my babyhood was for me. But I have done as much as I have been able to do to capture the way my mind worked when I was an infant—and, in many ways, still works now—and what I felt and experienced in those early days and months.

Yes, *Puddin': The Autobiography of a Baby* is fiction, but I believe it contains a true picture of who that baby was and what he went through—and how he got the groundings that made it possible to go forward into life sustained by deep hope.

A word of explanation

The language I created for the baby in this memoir employs, with two exceptions, single syllable words. For this reason, I needed to shorten the names of the key figures. Aunt is my Aunt Mary Reardon, later Mary Fitzgerald. And, yes, she did call me Puddin'. Gram is my mother's mother Grandma Mary Thomas, and Paw is her husband, my grandfather, Howard. They are all gone now.

Acknowledgements

Thanks to Thomas Pace, Patricia Cloud, Melanie Villines, Jeff Seitzer, Robert K. Elder, Paul Fericano, and Joan Servatius, and with special thanks to Julie Coplon.